COLOURS
of SUFFOLK

Mark Staples

HALSGROVE

To Eleanor, Maddie and Freddie

Acknowledgements

Peter Cross

Dean Staples

I would like to thank the following for kindly granting permission to publish
my photos, or for answering queries to aid me in the writing of the captions:

Angel Hotel, Bury St Edmunds

Mark Barnard, Suffolk County Council

Clare Priory

The National Trust Photo Library

Patrick Phillips, Kentwell Hall, Long Melford

Richard Storer, Baylham House Rare Breeds Farm

Lady Xa Tollemache, Helmingham Hall and Gardens

Adrian Walters, Sudbury Common Lands Charity

Disclaimer

*Whilst every care has been taken to ensure the accuracy of the captions to accompany
the images in this book, any errors or omissions will be corrected in future editions.*

Front cover: Village green, Monks Eleigh.
Back cover: Southwold beach huts.
Title page: Cottages lining the main street in the village of Kersey.

First published in Great Britain in 2018

Copyright © Mark Staples 2018

British Library Cataloguing-in-Publication Data
A CIP record for this title is available from the British Library

ISBN 978 0 85704 326 9

HALSGROVE

Halsgrove House,
Ryelands Business Park,
Bagley Road, Wellington, Somerset TA21 9PZ
Tel: 01823 653777   Fax: 01823 216796
email: sales@halsgrove.com

Part of the Halsgrove group of companies
Information on all Halsgrove titles is available at: www.halsgrove.com

Printed and bound in India by Parksons Graphics

Introduction

Suffolk is a county alive with colour. Situated in East Anglia, it offers miles of stunning coastline where colourful boats sail its waters and multi-coloured, wooden huts line its beaches. It has acres of beautiful countryside where colours change with the seasons. It boasts numerous historic towns and villages with pretty, pastel cottages and brightly painted landmarks. These seascapes, landscapes and landmarks all combine to create a fabulous palette of colours just waiting to be photographed.

Unsurprisingly, the vast majority of the Suffolk coast has been designated as an Area of Outstanding Natural Beauty. The towns dotted along the coastline are popular holiday destinations and are reminiscent of the seaside of yesteryear. Southwold with its golden, sandy beaches and its entertaining pier is much loved by families, whereas Aldeburgh with its shingle beach, fishing boats and festivals is the perfect spot for those interested in the coast's cultural heritage. However, what the Suffolk coast gives, nature is at times inclined to take away; the once large, thriving port of Dunwich was reclaimed by the North Sea, leaving the tiny, fishing village we see today.

The county is famed for its flat landscapes and big skies. Agriculture is an important industry here and just under half of Suffolk's farmland is devoted to cereal crops. Colourful fields of wheat, barley, rapeseed and sugar beet are a common sight and the occasional sunflower or poppy field is a rambler's delight. The natural environment is in abundance here; the woods, heathland and marshland of its many nature reserves provide vital habitat to some of the UK's rarest wildlife.

Suffolk's towns and villages are undeniably rich in history. Bury St Edmunds in the west of the county became home to the remains of the martyred King Edmund of the East Angles, killed in the ninth century by invading Danes. Around his shrine grew one of England's largest and wealthiest Benedictine abbeys, the ruins of which can still be found in the town today. Many Suffolk towns and villages made their fortunes on the back of the wool trade in the Middle Ages. Lavenham is perhaps the most famous wool town and is acknowledged as one of the best-preserved medieval settlements in England.

Colours of Suffolk offers a photographic journey around this beautiful county and gives just a hint of what is in store for visitors. Indeed, Suffolk has plenty to cater for every taste, covering the full spectrum in terms of both colour and interest. It is hoped that this book will inspire those who do not know the county to make a visit and that it will provide the residents of Suffolk with a source of pride.

Mark Staples
www.markstaples.co.uk

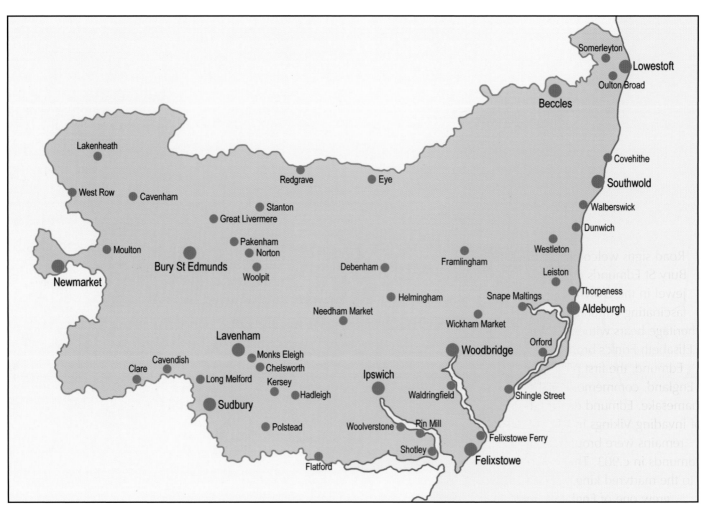

The main towns and villages featured in *Colours of Suffolk*.

Road signs welcoming visitors to Bury St Edmunds describe it as 'a jewel in the crown of Suffolk'. Its fascinating cultural and historical heritage bears witness to this. Dame Elisabeth Frink's bronze statue of St Edmund, the first patron saint of England, commemorates the town's namesake. Edmund died at the hands of invading Vikings in AD 869 and his remains were brought to Bury St Edmunds in c.903. This led to a shrine to the martyred king, around which grew one of England's most impressive Benedictine abbeys.

Ipswich is the county town of Suffolk and one of England's oldest towns. Once the civic hub, Ipswich Town Hall is located on Cornhill, in the bustling heart of the town. Its elaborate Victorian façade features sculptures of King Richard I, Cardinal Wolsey and King John, all of whom are important names in Ipswich's history. Today, Ipswich Town Hall houses two art galleries showcasing the work of local artists, a tea shop and function rooms for hire.

Once an important Saxon port, the small town of Beccles lies on the River Waveney in the very north of the county. The town boasts a weekly market, a farmers' market and a variety of independent boutiques, cafés and restaurants. Beccles is not without historical interest: Lord Horatio Nelson's parents, Catherine Suckling and Edmund Nelson, were married in St Michael's church in 1749.

These seafront houses add a splash of colour against the shingle in the coastal town of Aldeburgh. Unspoilt by commercialism, Aldeburgh is reminiscent of the seaside of yesteryear. Eateries, pubs, boutiques and galleries line its high street and the two family-run chip shops fry some of the tastiest fish and chips on the east coast, best enjoyed sitting on the beach looking out to the North Sea.

Stanton Windmill is a fine example of a post mill; its whole body is rotated on a central post to ensure that the sails are in the optimal position for the wind. It is one of a decreasing number of functioning post mills in the UK. It was built in 1751 and has been at its current location since 1818. After a long period of neglect, work began in 2004 that led to the restoration of this beautiful Grade II*-listed corn mill.

A visit to Lavenham in the heart of Suffolk is like stepping back in time. The town has countless timber-framed buildings to discover and is often referred to as the best-preserved medieval town in England. Lavenham owes its success to its once-thriving wool trade, more notably to the export of its famous blue broadcloth, and by the early 1520s it was the fourteenth-wealthiest town in the country.

The Tide Mill on the River Deben has become an iconic symbol of the town of Woodbridge. It is one of the first mills of its kind in the UK, as records show that a tide mill has been located here since 1170. The current Grade I-listed mill was built in 1793 and despite periods of inactivity throughout its lifetime, the mill has thankfully been restored to its former working glory.

Cavendish nestles in the Stour Valley and it is not hard to understand why it is often pictured in tourist guides about Suffolk. Thatched cottages and pastel-coloured houses line the main road that runs through the village. Cavendish is proud of its strong community spirit; its local store, the Duck or Grouse, is run mainly by volunteers and claims to be Britain's oldest shop.

Sudbury on the Suffolk-Essex border is perhaps best known as the birthplace of Thomas Gainsborough, the celebrated landscape and portrait painter. From an early age Gainsborough enjoyed drawing and painting Sudbury's glorious countryside. This bronze statue of the painter stands in pride of place on Market Hill in the centre of the historic wool town and was sculpted in 1913 by Sir Bertram Mackennal.

This statue of Hyperion, an acclaimed racehorse and stallion, stands in the centre of Newmarket. With over 350 years of racing history, Newmarket is acknowledged as the home of British horseracing. Just a stone's throw away from the statue lies the fascinating National Heritage Centre for Horseracing and Sporting Art, that was officially opened by Queen Elizabeth II in 2016 and was over ten years in the making.

There are few seaside towns with as much timeless charm as Southwold. Its golden, sandy beaches, colourful beach huts and nineteenth-century lighthouse all contribute to this charm and its entertaining pier makes Southwold a popular destination with families. It is one of many resorts along the 50 miles of glorious Suffolk Heritage Coast, making it a suitable base from which to explore the area further.

Captain's Wood is set in the village of Sudbourne near Woodbridge and in spring offers arguably the most spectacular display of bluebells in the county. This ancient woodland provides important habitat for barn owls, grass snakes, deer and several species of bat and is one of many nature reserves in the county managed by Suffolk Wildlife Trust.

Dunwich Heath undergoes a remarkable transformation in summer, when the heather and gorse bloom, creating a vibrant carpet of purples, pinks and yellows as far as the eye can see. This stretch of the Suffolk coast is home to rare wildlife, including the woodlark and the Dartford warbler. It is managed by the National Trust and offers magnificent cliff-top views and excellent walks, whatever the season, in this Area of Outstanding Natural Beauty.

The 'splash' is a ford running through Kersey, undeniably one of the prettiest villages in Suffolk. The red-bricked façade of Ye Olde River House overlooks the ford and just yards away, the timber-framed, fourteenth-century Bell Inn offers a superb menu of traditional pub fare. Like many towns and villages nearby, Kersey prospered in the Middle Ages thanks to the wool trade and it is famed for the woollen cloth to which it gave its name.

Saxtead Green Windmill is a well-loved post mill in the village of Saxtead and is believed to date to the eighteenth century. Records suggest, however, that a corn mill has been located here since the late thirteenth century. Whilst the mill is still in good working condition, it has not operated commercially since 1947. It is under the care of English Heritage.

Left: This gateway leads to Framlingham Mere, a fantastic vantage point from which to admire the imposing twelfth-century English castle. Built between 1189 and 1200, Framlingham Castle has a colourful history; a plaque on the castle wall reveals that Mary Tudor was proclaimed Queen here in 1553 amidst a succession crisis. Today, an exciting family day out beckons at this popular English Heritage attraction, that in 2017 became the subject of an Ed Sheeran song recollecting his childhood memories.

Right: Once a small, tranquil fishing village on the Suffolk coast called Thorpe, Thorpeness is today a magical, vibrant holiday destination. Following serious flooding in the village in 1910, its owner, Glencairn Stuart Ogilvie, came up with the idea of transforming it into a fantasy holiday resort for his family and friends. His dream was realised just a few years later in the form of a themed boating lake, mock-Tudor houses and a 70-foot water tower disguised as a fairy-tale house in the sky.

Polstead owes its name, 'place by the pools', to the ponds at the foot of the village hill. It lies on the edge of the Stour Valley and is notorious for the legendary Red Barn Murder. Maria Marten and her lover, William Corder, met in the Red Barn in May 1827 with the intention of eloping. It was here that Corder killed Marten, before taking flight. He sent letters to her family claiming that all was well with the couple, but her father discovered her body a year later, leading to Corder's trial and hanging in Bury St Edmunds.

Moyse's Hall Museum in Bury St Edmunds exhibits relics connected to the Red Barn Murder. These include Corder's scalp, a copy of his death bust and a book recounting the murder bound in his skin. Moyse's Hall became a local history museum just before the turn of the twentieth century. Prior to this, it had housed the town's gaol, workhouse and police station. It stands on Cornhill, overlooking the town's twice-weekly market.

Its location on the River Orwell made Pin Mill the ideal haunt for smugglers. The smugglers are long gone, but little else has changed in this charming hamlet. It is an idyllic starting point for stimulating nature walks along the River Orwell, whatever the season. Houseboats can be discovered along the way: some are still inhabited, whilst others have long been deserted and lie derelict.

Chelsworth lies in the Brett Valley in the south of the county and has understandably been categorised as a conservation area. The road that meanders through the village is bordered by enchanting cottages. The fourteenth-century church and the half-timbered village inn add to its beauty. In 2017, Chelsworth celebrated its fiftieth Open Gardens, a concept that is believed to have originated in the village and that has since been replicated throughout the country.

Once a flourishing fishing port on the River Ore, Orford is today a small, serene village with a pretty quay to discover. Fishing boats and yachts now share the quay with boats offering trips to explore the sights along the river, such as Havergate Island Nature Reserve, Suffolk's only island. Pinney's of Orford sells its renowned smoked fish from its shop on the quay. Its logo depicts the legendary 'Merman of Orford', said to have been caught in fishermen's nets in the second half of the twelfth century.

Located on the southern point of the Broads National Park, Oulton Broad is the perfect place to enjoy water sports of all kinds. Exploring the River Waveney on a passenger or hired boat is also an exciting option. Situated just outside the popular holiday destination of Lowestoft, Oulton Broad has its fair share of eateries, pubs and shops and its Edwardian park is a firm family favourite in the summer months.

Somerleyton in the north of the county has a timeless appeal. Its village green is bordered by these unusual, but beautiful thatched cottages. However, the village is perhaps better known for Somerleyton Hall, its grand Tudor-Jacobean-style stately home and gardens that open to visitors from April to September every year.

The hamlet of Flatford in the scenic Dedham Vale provided inspiration to one of Britain's greatest painters, John Constable. Bridge Cottage, pictured here overlooking the River Stour, appears in some of his paintings and is just a stone's throw away from the famous Flatford Mill, once owned by his father. The landscape portrayed in Constable's works is affectionately known as Constable Country and is unsurprisingly an Area of Outstanding Natural Beauty.

Felixstowe Seafront Gardens offer an attractive setting for a leisurely stroll along the promenade. The Grade II-listed gardens were created in Victorian times, when visiting the coast for its health benefits became fashionable. *The Willow Family Sculpture*, beautifully crafted by Tracy Barritt-Brown, evokes nostalgia for this bygone era. The gardens extend for a kilometre along the seafront, earning the town the title of 'the Garden Resort of East Anglia'.

The leaning cottage of Cordwainers is one of the most photographed buildings on the High Street of the medieval town of Lavenham and is the source of much wonderment amongst visitors. Records show that this fifteenth-century property was formerly the One Bell Inn, whilst its current name suggests that it once served as a shoemaker's.

The ruins of one of the UK's wealthiest and most important Benedictine monasteries lie in the centre of the market town of Bury St Edmunds. The Abbey was formed in 1020 after the remains of the martyred King Edmund were brought to the site in c.903, transforming it into a shrine and a popular place of pilgrimage. The beautiful ruins are quite substantial and offer a clear indication of the size of these once awe-inspiring Abbey precincts.

The Walled Kitchen Garden with its colourful herbaceous borders, vegetable plots and tunnelled walkways is one of many to explore at Helmingham Hall. The spectacular Grade I-listed gardens are set in 400 acres of deer-inhabited parkland and have been shaped by Xa Tollemache, award-winning garden designer and Lady of the magnificent Tudor manor. Helmingham Hall was the winner of the 2017 Historic Houses Association Garden of the Year Award.

Agriculture is a major industry in Suffolk, employing over 8200 people. Nearly half of all farmland here is used for growing cereals, such as barley and wheat, although rapeseed and sugar beet are also commonly cultivated crops. Pig farming is an equally significant area of activity in the county, as over a fifth of the country's pork from outdoor-reared pigs comes from Suffolk.

Despite the two monks on its village sign, the pretty village of Monks Eleigh has never actually had a monastery. Its name stems from the monks of Canterbury, who owned much of the property in the village until the Dissolution of the Monasteries. The monks are said to have provided a priest for the village church of St Peter and it is likely that they contributed financially to the construction of the beautiful church we see there today.

Southwold is a definite contender for the title of 'Beach-hut Capital of England'. The colourful, wooden huts are large in number and have an equally large price tag. Some sell for as much as £150,000 and, despite this, they are still very much in demand. Thankfully, some are available to hire directly through the proprietor.

Lucky visitors to the county might encounter a sunflower field whilst exploring the Suffolk countryside in summer. This beautiful field was discovered near West Stow.

Shotley Marina is a peaceful place to sit and watch the world go by. Visitors often enjoy seeing the coming and going of sailing boats via the marina lock, before retiring to the Shipwreck pub to sample its food and drink. Until 1976, Shotley was home to HMS *Ganges*, where more than 150,000 Navy cadets were trained. A fascinating museum in the marina traces its history. For several years, police cadets were also trained here.

This fifteenth-century packhorse bridge crosses the River Kennett in the pretty village of Moulton on the Suffolk-Cambridgeshire border. Made of stone rubble and flint, the bridge has four pointed, brick-lined arches and is just over 65 feet in length. It formed part of the old route between Bury St Edmunds and Cambridge.

Dwellings of all shades border the streets of the picturesque village of Pakenham, like this seventeenth-century house that was once a village pub called the Bell Inn. Located roughly 6 miles to the east of Bury St Edmunds, Pakenham has both a working watermill and a working windmill, earning it the title of the 'Village of Two Mills'.

St Andrew's church in the coastal village of Covehithe is unique. The church was originally built in the fifteenth century, but villagers were struggling to maintain it two centuries later. This led to the building of a smaller church within the existing one. Materials from the medieval church were used in its construction, resulting in this beautiful, striking shell we see today. Sadly, locals fear that coastal erosion will one day see the church reclaimed by the sea.

Walberswick is a small village on the Suffolk coast where time appears to have stood still. With its sandy beaches and a full list of village amenities, it is a well-loved holiday resort. Walberswick is renowned for crabbing and the harbour is packed with families equipped with their lines and buckets in the summer months. Southwold sits on the opposite bank of the River Blyth, pictured here, where wooden shacks sell fish caught earlier that day.

The Almshouses in Thorpeness were originally constructed as homes for the workers in Glencairn Stuart Ogilvie's fantasy holiday village in 1926. Like many of the village's buildings, they are mock Tudor. Today, the Almshouses are retirement homes.

Cattle pose for the camera at Redgrave and Lopham Fen. This National Nature Reserve is managed by Suffolk Wildlife Trust and was formed through human activity over many years. Peat digging and the management of reeds for use in thatching contributed to a habitat in which wetland species thrived. After the war, the area was drained and much of the fen dried out, but fortunately, it was saved and is once again rich in plant life, including native carnivorous plants such as sundew and butterwort, as well as wildlife like the Fen Raft Spider, the UK's largest spider.

Southwold is not the only Suffolk town with multi-coloured beach huts. Several rows of these wooden structures stretch along the sea wall between Old Felixstowe and Felixstowe Ferry, creating a cheerful backdrop for a gentle walk. A couple of historic Martello Towers can also be found en route, built to provide protection in the event of an invasion by Napoleon.

Situated on the River Stour, the historic wool town of Clare is Suffolk's smallest town. It has an abundance of wonderful old houses, some dating from Tudor times. Clare has many visitor attractions that include the thirteenth-century priory, the beautiful Gothic church of St Peter and St Paul and its neighbouring Ancient House Museum. As its name suggests, the 33-acre Clare Castle Country Park is home to the ruins of Clare Castle. The former railway station is also located there.

Suffolk's climate is predominantly mild, but the odd snowy day is a photographer's delight and a rare opportunity to catch some of the county's famous landmarks under a white blanket. Pictured here are Cathedral Grounds in Bury St Edmunds, flanked by the Norman Tower, the Great Church Yard and, of course, the Cathedral itself.

Once the largest enclosed dock in the UK, the Victorian wet dock in Ipswich has evolved into a vibrant, contemporary waterfront. The extensive, on-going regeneration programme has led to several chic restaurants, bars, cafés and boutiques, as well as these attractive apartments overlooking the moored boats on Neptune Quay. The dock is home to the University of Suffolk and DanceEast, an acclaimed organisation playing a key role in the promotion of dance in the East of England.

Helmingham Hall is a striking, moated Tudor hall near Stowmarket and has been home to the Tollemache family for over five hundred years. The house is not open to the public, but its exceptional gardens can be visited between May and September every year. An afternoon or cream tea in the Coach House Tea Rooms is a pleasant way to conclude this English garden experience.

Golden straw bales are a common sight in the Suffolk landscape from the end of August to the beginning of September. These were photographed on the Shotley peninsula near Ipswich.

Bury St Edmunds in West Suffolk is surrounded by many rural villages, like Fornham All Saints to the northwest of the town. As well as pretty thatched cottages, it has two golf courses and a beautiful church, parts of which date to the thirteenth century. It claims to be the site of the only recorded set-piece battle in Suffolk, where thousands of rebel soldiers fought and died in 1173, as they attempted to bring down Henry II.

Westleton Heath lies on the east coast in the Sandlings, so called due to its sandy soil. It is a National Nature Reserve where the bright purples and pinks of heather dominate the vast and open landscape in the summer months. The heather plays an important role in providing nectar for the butterflies and other invertebrates, whereas the open scrubland is the ideal environment for the nightjar and the stonechat.

Orfordness Lighthouse was built in 1792 and stands 30 metres tall on Orford Ness, an important National Trust nature reserve with an extraordinary military past. The shingle spit provides a unique habitat to many internationally rare species of flora and fauna, but for over seventy years, top-secret military experiments took place here. Some of its deserted test buildings, many of which lie derelict, are still there to be explored.

Flatford Mill is undoubtedly the centrepiece of the sleepy hamlet of Flatford in the picturesque countryside of the Dedham Vale. It once belonged to John Constable's father and it is from and around this mill that Constable painted some of his most famous works, including *The Hay Wain* and *Boat Building near Flatford Mill*. Willy Lott's cottage, visible in some of Constable's paintings, lies just across the mill pond.

These South Devon Cattle wander freely in the summer months through the Common Lands of the historic market town of Sudbury. It is thought that cattle have grazed on these ancient water meadows for more than a millennium. They share the common with the locals, who come here to enjoy the serenity of this splendid scenery. The arrival of autumn sees the departure of the cattle and the saturation of the flood plain in this ever-changing landscape.

The Swan at Lavenham is amongst Suffolk's finest hotels and is one of over 340 listed buildings in this magnificent medieval town. Once a fifteenth-century inn, its beautiful timber-framed building has evolved into what it describes as a stylish luxury hotel and spa. The Swan's Airmen's Bar pays homage to the US airmen based in Lavenham during the Second World War.

Beccles Quay lies in the most southerly part of the Broads National Park. A boat trip on the River Waveney offers captivating views of the Southern Broads and the surrounding Suffolk countryside. Boats are available to hire for the day, or visitors can book the Big Dog Ferry to Geldeston Locks Inn, just over the Norfolk border. Alternatively, a walk along the river to discover Beccles Marshes is an equally enjoyable possibility.

Clare Priory is amongst the earliest religious houses in the country. It owes its beginnings to Richard de Clare, who invited the Augustinian Friars to England in 1248 to set up their first priory. Following the Reformation and consequent suppression of the Priory, it had various owners for over four centuries, until the Augustinians returned to their original home in 1953.

The Suffolk coast has a wide choice of sand or shingle beaches to enjoy. The shingle beach at Dunwich is a pleasant spot for an invigorating coastal walk. The tiny village was once a large port, before being engulfed by the North Sea many years ago. Legend has it that during bad weather, the haunting sound of church bells tolling can be heard beneath the sea, supposedly announcing the arrival of a storm.

The imposing Norman Tower in Bury St Edmunds was once the main entrance to the Abbey church. Constructed between 1120 and 1148, it is reputed to be England's oldest Norman building. It houses the bells of the neighbouring St Edmundsbury Cathedral and is maintained by English Heritage.

This beautiful, brick and timber-framed exterior belongs to Moot Hall in Aldeburgh. Now a local history museum, this sixteenth-century building has an interesting past. In the seventeenth century, Witch Finder General Matthew Hopkins was employed to seek out witches in Aldeburgh. As a result, seven so-called witches were imprisoned in Moot Hall and hanged in 1646.

Orford Castle was built between 1165 and 1173 by Henry II to guard against coastal invasion and to increase his presence in the county. All that remains today is its polygonal keep, still in remarkable condition and very worthy of a visit. Managed by English Heritage, the keep contains an impressive local history museum and its rooftop affords fantastic views over the village and Orford Ness Nature Reserve.

Southwold Lighthouse towers 31 metres above the surrounding houses in the town centre of this seaside resort. The Grade II-listed lighthouse we see today began operating in 1890 and was automated in 1938 when electricity was installed. Southwold was once home to the English author George Orwell, who wrote *A Clergyman's Daughter* whilst resident there. His family home, Montague House, is situated on the High Street, a ten-minute walk from the lighthouse.

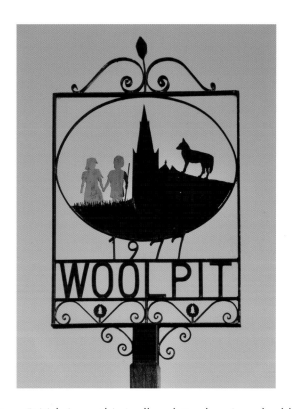

A true British icon, this Ludlow letter box is embedded in the wall of the old Woolpit Post Office. Just yards away, the village sign portrays the intriguing story of the 'Green Children of Woolpit'. In the twelfth century, two children with green skin were allegedly discovered in wolf pits near St Mary's church. They spoke an incomprehensible language and would eat nothing but beans. The boy became ill and sadly died. The girl eventually adapted to her new surroundings, lost the green tinge and learnt to speak English.

Comprising little more than a row of coastguard cottages, a few houses and a Martello Tower, Shingle Street is an isolated, coastal retreat. The Martello Tower is one of a number that were built to defend the country from a possible attack by Napoleon. This stretch of coastline is home to much wildlife. Plants such as sea kale and viper's bugloss grow on the shingle beach and the grasshopper warbler breeds on the marshland.

Village signs are often used to mark a celebration or special event. Debenham's sign was erected to celebrate Queen Elizabeth II's Silver Jubilee and it reflects the historic importance of the wool trade in the area. The discovery of Roman coins in Debenham and its entry in the Domesday Book of 1086 are testament to the town's long history and it claims to have had one of the first purpose-built police stations in the UK.

In the midst of the bustling Ipswich Waterfront stands the Old Custom House, a nod to the historic importance of the former wet dock. The elegant Victorian building is now the premises of the Ipswich Port Authority. Nearby, the Ipswich Maritime Museum Window on Albion Quay offers a unique insight into the heritage of this regenerated dock that extends for one kilometre along the edge of Ipswich town.

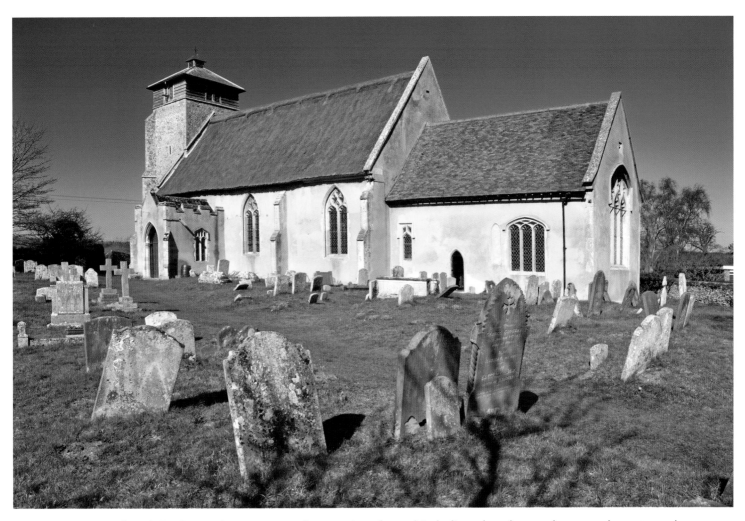

St Peter's church in Great Livermere stands on a site of worship believed to date to the seventh century; the Domesday Book records that 'a church with 12 acres of land, 10 furlongs long by 8 furlongs wide, paying 12d in geld' stood here. In the atmospheric churchyard, a gravestone marks the resting place of William Sakings, falconer to Charles I and II, and James II. M. R. James, the well-known writer credited with the invention of the English ghost story, spent his childhood in the rectory here and is also commemorated in the church.

Sheep graze on either side of the tree-lined driveway that leads to Ipswich High School in Woolverstone. The school is housed in the beautiful Woolverstone Hall and is situated on the River Orwell in 80 acres of parkland. 'Cat House' near Woolverstone Marina was allegedly the home of the infamous Margaret Catchpole and her lover, William Laud. It is said that she placed a white china cat in a window of the house to assist Laud and his fellow smugglers in avoiding customs men.

Thorpeness Meare is the focal point of Glencairn Stuart Ogilvie's fantasy holiday village. The shallow boating lake was inspired by *Peter Pan,* whose creator, J. M. Barrie, was a close acquaintance of Ogilvie. The *Neverland* theme is therefore reflected all over the Meare, making this a popular attraction for children. Colourful rowing boats are available for hire and share the lake with swans and other waterfowl.

Once a functioning watermill, the Mill Hotel in Sudbury sits on the edge of the town's enchanting water meadows and overlooks the beautiful mill pond, home to these swans. It is believed that a mill has been situated here for over a thousand years. Today, the Mill Hotel is an excellent location for enjoying a drink outdoors on a balmy summer evening, whilst taking in the stunning scenery and listening to the soothing water of the mill pond.

The white-washed, half-timbered Guildhall of Corpus Christi offers a fascinating historical insight into the people who made Lavenham the place it is today. The growth of the woollen cloth trade led to its construction in around 1530, as was the case for many of the town's grand buildings. Throughout its history, the building has seen many uses; it has been a place of worship, a gaol, a public house and has even served as a hang-out for American servicemen during the Second World War.

Covered in Boston ivy, the Angel Hotel is a striking Grade II*-listed building. Originally a Georgian coaching inn, the four-star hotel describes itself today as 'a contemporary boutique hotel set in the heart of historic Bury St Edmunds'. Charles Dickens is perhaps the Angel's most famous guest. He is thought to have stayed in the hotel on three separate occasions and chose to include the Angel in *The Pickwick Papers*. The present-day Room 215 was his preferred room and is still furnished with the original four-poster bed where he slept.

Historically a small fishing village, Aldeburgh had become a flourishing port by the sixteenth century and enjoyed a successful shipbuilding industry. Sir Francis Drake's *Golden Hind* came from its shipyards. As its significance as a port gradually waned, it came to depend upon fishing once more. Colourful fishing boats are still active here today, albeit reduced in number, and are commonly seen on the pebbled beach surrounded by their nets and other paraphernalia after a morning at sea.

The small fishing hamlet of Felixstowe Ferry has an old-world charm. Wooden sheds near the boatyard sell fresh fish supplied by local fishermen, whose boats lie at anchor on the River Deben. A foot and bicycle ferry operates across the river between Felixstowe Ferry and Bawdsey; families are often seen crabbing along the jetty that leads to the ferry's departure point. The Ferry Boat Inn, the Ferry Café and Winkles at the Ferry all ensure that visitors will never go hungry.

Colourful shops, cafés, and restaurants share the lively village of Wickham Market with the beautiful All Saints' church and its octagonal tower, a pretty watermill and a monthly market on Market Hill. The charming village is a convenient base from which to visit other nearby Suffolk towns and villages, such as Framlingham, Woodbridge and Orford.

Holy Trinity church in the village of Long Melford is one of the longest and most awe-inspiring churches in Suffolk. The fifteenth-century edifice owes its grandeur to the prosperity stemming from Suffolk's medieval wool trade. The current tower, pictured here, was built at the turn of the twentieth century around a Georgian tower that had been added when the original one was struck by lightning.

At the foot of Southwold Lighthouse, the Sole Bay Inn serves beers, wines and spirits from Adnams Brewery, just yards away. A visit to the pub is a must for beer enthusiasts, as it offers up to six Adnams cask ales at any given time. Wholesome pub classics are cooked and served daily.

The short walk from the quay into Orford village centre reveals these chocolate-box cottages. These are not the only highlights to be found along the way. At the top of the hill lies St Bartholomew's, a beautiful church with Norman remnants. In the village centre, Orford's shops, pubs and restaurants have a timeless appeal, like the award-winning Pump Street Bakery. However, the village's most notable attraction has to be its twelfth-century castle.

Needham Lake in Mid Suffolk is a beautiful spot for a Sunday afternoon stroll and is particularly attractive in autumn, when the trees around the water's edge begin to reveal their vibrant colours. It is a much-loved destination for families due to the picnic areas, children's playgrounds, and ducks to feed. Fishing is a popular activity here too.

Monks Eleigh is one of many pretty villages in the Brett Valley in the heart of Suffolk. The village green with its historic pump is surrounded by quaint cottages and is overlooked by the parish church of St Peter. The church tower affords superb views over the whole village. The thatched Swan Inn also stands on the edge of the green and offers a varied menu prepared using local, seasonal produce.

It is easy to understand why Pin Mill on the Shotley peninsula is a popular haunt for photographers and artists. The views are second to none. The Butt and Oyster public house is the ideal place to take in these views, whilst enjoying a pint and a varied food menu. This popular pub owes its name to the oyster fisheries, once a significant enterprise here. *We Didn't Mean To Go To Sea,* the seventh book in Arthur Ransome's *Swallows and Amazons* series, was set in Pin Mill.

Unsurprisingly, Market Place in Lavenham has often been used as the backdrop for television dramas or films. Simply remove all the twenty-first-century vehicles to reveal an impeccable medieval setting. Areas of Lavenham, including the Market Cross pictured here on the left, can be seen in the film *Harry Potter and the Deathly Hallows Part 1*. The Market Cross also witnessed public executions in times gone by.

The Great Gate, or Abbey Gate as it is known locally, provides a grand entrance to the Abbey Gardens in the heart of historic Bury St Edmunds. It originally led to the Great Court of the Benedictine Abbey that once stood on this site. Relations between the townsfolk and the Abbey were at best tense, leading to the riots of 1327 and the destruction of the original gate. The gate we see standing proud on Angel Hill today was rebuilt around 1347.

Come rain or shine, Aldeburgh is the perfect destination to take in the beauty and tranquillity of the east coast. A walk along the seafront to neighbouring Thorpeness and back is guaranteed to blow away the cobwebs. It is easy to see why composer Benjamin Britten was so enamoured with this stretch of shoreline.

Lines of trees border both banks of the River Brett in the ancient market town of Hadleigh, making this a particularly attractive setting to enjoy a spot of angling. Hadleigh was once a wool town, but a decline in the wool trade led sadly to its demise. Thankfully, the advent of the railway in Victorian times saw its fortunes change. Many of the houses in the town reflect this history and are a mixture of medieval buildings with Victorian façades.

Any visitor to the county cannot fail to notice the numerous 'Suffolk-pink' buildings dotted around its towns and villages, like this charming cottage that stands on the driveway leading to Clare Priory. The colour originated in the fourteenth century and was achieved by mixing natural ingredients such as elderberries, red earth or even pig's blood into the limewash or plaster.

Located on the west bank of the River Deben in the Suffolk Coast and Heaths Area of Outstanding Natural Beauty, the rural village of Waldringfield is an idyllic spot to escape from it all. Patrons of the Maybush Inn can take in the scenic river views and watch the yachts of the local sailing club go by, whilst sampling the excellent menu of this former fourteenth-century farmhouse.

The aptly named House in the Clouds was once a water tower in the guise of a magical cottage and provided water for Thorpeness, Glencairn Stuart Ogilvie's fantasy holiday village. The 70-foot folly has since been converted into a real house, offering quirky holiday accommodation and sparking much amazement amongst visitors to this vibrant resort on the Suffolk Heritage Coast.

Suffolk-pink cottages stand between the village green and the medieval church of St Mary the Virgin, creating this classic picture-postcard view of Cavendish. The village green was declared 'liveliest in the country' in 2010 by the *Sunday Telegraph, Life*, a well-deserved accolade given the abundance and popularity of events held there. From plant fayres to vintage car displays, the list is endless.

Suffolk's last working watermill can be found in the village of Pakenham. Although the current mill dates to the eighteenth century, flour has been produced here for around a thousand years. The mill was purchased by the Suffolk Building Preservation Trust in 1978 and a group of volunteers is responsible for its everyday running. Pakenham is unique in that it also boasts a working windmill, hence its title of 'Village of Two Mills'.

With its 940 planks from beginning to end, Southwold Pier stretches 623 feet into the North Sea. Built at the turn of the twentieth century, the original structure was 810 feet in length, but years of storms, rebuilds and renovations by various owners have led to the pier we see today. Its decks offer gift shops, eateries and much family fun, with attractions such as the House of Games, the Wacky Walk of Mirrors, and Tim Hunkin and Will Jackson's Waterclock, to name just a few.

The tower of Suffolk's only cathedral rises 150 feet or so above the Rose Garden of the Abbey Gardens in Bury St Edmunds. Constructed within the Benedictine Abbey precincts, St Edmundsbury Cathedral grew from the parish church of St James. It became a cathedral in 1914, and although parts of its building date to the sixteenth century, its spectacular tower was added at the turn of the millennium.

Snape Maltings is acknowledged as a world-class centre for music and was the brainchild of Suffolk-born composer Benjamin Britten. Its extensive programme of concerts and events includes the renowned Aldeburgh Festival. The whole complex, including its shops, eateries and galleries, is housed in revamped industrial buildings from the Victorian era. Its setting amongst the reed beds and marshes by the River Alde makes Snape Maltings an alluring spot for walkers and nature enthusiasts.

Suffolk has a large choice of picture-postcard village pubs, like the Dog in Norton in Mid Suffolk. This popular seventeenth-century inn boasts an open fireplace and oak beams and has varied menus of freshly prepared dishes using locally and regionally sourced ingredients. It is proud to offer a gluten-free menu and serves fine beers supplied by the Greene King Brewery in nearby Bury St Edmunds.

This Lavenham house displays a fine specimen of pargeting, ornamental plasterwork typically applied to the façades of buildings. The craft has existed for centuries and is prevalent in Suffolk and other areas of East Anglia to this day. One of the most renowned and impressive examples of pargeting in the county can be found on the Ancient House in Ipswich.

Fresh growth is a sign that spring is here at Orwell Country Park, spanning around 250 acres on the banks of the River Orwell near Ipswich. Ancient woodland, heathland, scrubland and reed beds make up the park, part of which is set within the Suffolk Coast and Heaths Area of Outstanding Natural Beauty. It is managed by Ipswich Borough Council.

St Mary's in Pakenham is a beautiful, flint church with a number of distinctive characteristics; it is one of very few cruciform churches in Suffolk and the upper part of its central tower is unusually octagonal, but square below. The building still retains some of its original twelfth-century features, although the church has undergone considerable rebuilding and restoration over the years. All this adds to the interest of this pretty village church.

Suffolk comes second to neighbouring Norfolk for the greatest number of village signs. This eye-catching example in West Row is one of over 350 in Suffolk, whereas Norfolk boasts as many as 500. It is said that the tradition of decorative village signs owes its beginnings to Edward VII who, as the Prince of Wales, commissioned signs for villages on the Sandringham Estate in Norfolk.

At the beginning of the 1900s, as many as seventy fishing boats are thought to have operated from the shores of Aldeburgh. Today, fishermen still sell their early morning catch from the wooden shacks that line the beach, but the number of active boats has sadly dwindled. A few lie redundant on the shingle, but have been repainted by locals to serve as a reminder of this important part of the cultural heritage of the town.

The impressive St Edmundsbury Cathedral provides a magnificent backdrop to the award-winning Abbey Gardens in Bury St Edmunds. The park covers an area of 14 acres and can be found in the town centre where the Benedictine Abbey once stood, the ruins of which are still a prominent feature of the gardens. The River Lark, an aviary, a bowling green and a children's play area are just some of the attractions here, although nothing can top the exceptional floral displays of the gardens.

Buttrum's Windmill on the edge of Woodbridge is recognised as one of the country's most handsome tower mills. It has six storeys and was constructed in 1836 by John Whitmore, one of Suffolk's most renowned millwrights. It owes its name, however, to its last miller, George Buttrum, who ceased to operate the mill commercially in 1928.

The occasional sunflower field,
tucked away in the Suffolk landscape,
is always a pleasant find.

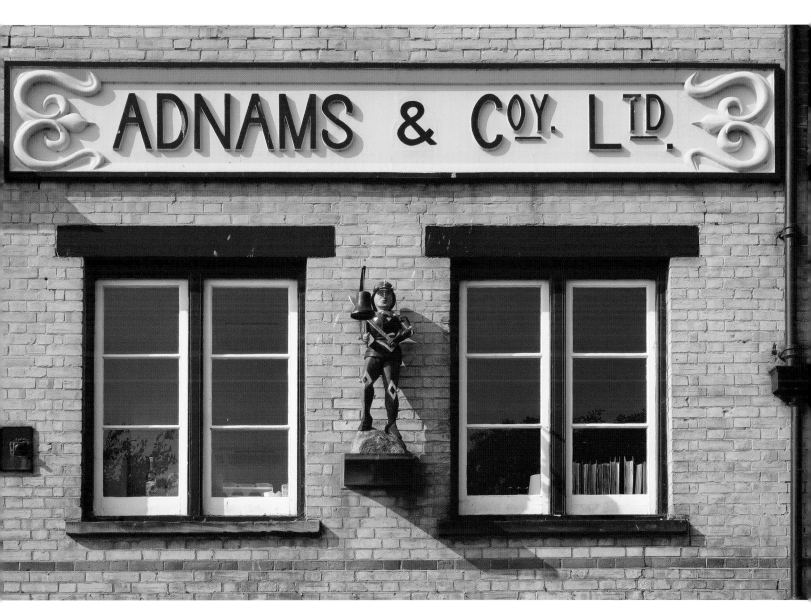

Adnams Brewery was founded in 1872, when George and Ernest Adnams purchased the Sole Bay Brewery in the beautiful seaside town of Southwold. Records reveal, however, that beer was brewed on this site as early as 1345. Although famed for its ales, Adnams distils its very own award-winning spirits, on sale at its many pubs and retail outlets throughout East Anglia. Visitors to the town should ensure that a brewery tour is on their itinerary.

Taking over three years to build, the Orwell Bridge opened in December 1982 to take the A45, now the A14, over the River Orwell near Ipswich. It spans 1.2 kilometres in total, making it one of the longest bridges in the country without a toll, and over 19,000 tonnes of steel were used in its construction.

Eye in North Suffolk boasts more listed buildings than the medieval town of Lavenham. A visit to the mound of Eye Castle reveals this classic view of the church of St Peter and St Paul, a predominantly fourteenth-century structure with an impressive fifteenth-century tower. Next to the church stands the former Guildhall, an iconic, black and white timber-framed building, possibly dating from the 1470s.

The grand church of St Peter and St Paul in Lavenham very much befits the status of a once prosperous wool town. It was indeed built by wealthy wool merchants between 1486 and 1525 and some would say that it is the prettiest of all Suffolk wool churches. Its fine, straight lines are in stark contrast to the many warped, timber-framed buildings elsewhere in the town.

Modern beach huts look over the golden sands of Lowestoft, the UK's most easterly town and the first spot in the country to experience sunrise. The celebrated composer, Benjamin Britten, was born in this once busy fishing port. Today, Lowestoft is a popular holiday destination, with all the typical amenities associated with the English seaside, such as fish and chip shops, piers and amusement arcades.

Located where Silent Street meets St Peter's Street, this beautiful bronze sculpture marks the life of Cardinal Thomas Wolsey, arguably Ipswich's most famous son. Wolsey was born in the town in around 1470 and went on to play a defining role in British history as Lord Chancellor to Henry VIII. The statue was sculpted by David Annand.

This distinctive black and white tower mill stands five storeys tall on the edge of Pakenham village and can be seen from miles around. Built in 1830, the mill has been in the care of the Bryant family since the 1880s and although it has not milled commercially since the 1970s, it is still in working order.

This is one of several pollarded willows displaying new growth on the banks of the River Stour in Sudbury's Common Lands. Pollarding is an ancient pruning technique for managing tree growth, involving the regular removal of branches above grazing height to leave just the trunk. This stopped livestock feeding off the fresh growth that would have been used for fuel or fences. Today, pollarding ensures that the trees remain strong and enjoy a long life.

Since purchasing Kentwell Hall in the 1970s, Patrick Phillips and his family have worked tirelessly to restore this moated Tudor Hall. Visitors will not be disappointed, as there is much to see both inside and out. Many rooms are open for public viewing and the extensive grounds contain beautiful gardens and a rare-breed farm. One of the highlights on Kentwell's busy programme of events includes annual Tudor re-enactments.

A small group of Konik Ponies has been used to graze Redgrave and Lopham Fen for over twenty years. These primitive, hardy, semi-wild horses from Poland are ideally suited to the wetland environment. Their preference for grazing on coarse grasses, sedges and rushes, while leaving many of the wildflower species untouched, makes them fitting allies of the Suffolk Wildlife Trust in promoting the rich diversity of plant life on this nationally important nature reserve.

The streets of Kersey are lined with pretty, colourful cottages. Many are thatched or half-timbered and at the height of the wool trade in medieval times, they were occupied by weaver families. Today, they are homes to the 350 or so residents of the village. At the top of the village hill sits St Mary's church, a beautiful building of stone and flint with an impressive tower, very much in keeping with other wool churches in the area.

This beautiful stained glass window can be found in the church of Clare Priory. It depicts St Thomas of Villanova, a Spanish friar of the Order of Saint Augustine. It was the Augustinians who came over to Clare and founded the Priory in the thirteenth century.

Built in 1884, the imposing red-bricked Hawks Mill stands by the River Gipping in the town of Needham Market. Once a corn-grinding watermill, the building is now an apartment block. Like many Suffolk towns, Needham Market played its role in the wool trade. Wool combing was its speciality, until its demise due to the plague at the beginning of the 1660s. Workers prepared the wool for weaving in combing sheds close to where the mill lies today.

Love it or hate it, Maggi Hambling's *Scallop* stands proud on the shingle beach in Aldeburgh. It pays tribute to the famous composer, Benjamin Britten, who lived in the town and cherished its coastline. The words 'I hear those voices that will not be drowned', taken from Britten's opera *Peter Grimes*, are cut out of the steel along the top edge of sculpture. *Scallop* was met with mixed reactions when it was installed in 2003.

Little Hall in Lavenham's Market Place was originally built as a clothier's house with the wealth generated by the medieval wool trade. Today, this fourteenth-century house with its pretty walled garden is a museum whose walls have a tale to tell; the rooms inside the house have evolved with the town and therefore reflect Lavenham's fascinating history.

The Town Hall in Eye in North Suffolk is a distinctive Victorian building of flint and brick. Its clock tower was once used as a gaol for local felons and to the rear of the building is the town's only pub, the Queen's Head. In Old English, Eye means 'island', suggesting that the town was historically enclosed by water. Today, the town's main attractions include its castle and its beautiful medieval church.

Arc shopping centre in Bury St Edmunds provides something of a contrast to the numerous historic buildings of the town. It describes itself as a 'modern street-scape centre' and boasts around forty shops and restaurants. The Apex, a first-class concert venue, can also be found in Arc. Its acoustics are second to none and its vast programme of events caters for all tastes.

Lines of contorted Scots pine trees define the landscape of the Brecks, an area covering approximately 390 square miles in Suffolk and Norfolk. Traditionally grown as hedges, the young, trimmed trees were suited to the dry soils here and protected the crops from the wind. Over time, they grew into the wind-gnarled specimens we see today. Unsurprisingly, the Brecks play a vital conservation role; in summer, they provide habitat for two-thirds of the country's rare stone curlews.

St Nicholas's church and Church Cottage create this classic view of the village of Rattlesden between Bury St Edmunds and Stowmarket. The enchanting timber-framed cottage is largely mid fifteenth century, whereas parts of St Nicholas's church predate this by roughly two hundred years. Both are amongst approximately 60 beautiful listed buildings in this officially-designated conservation area.

Woodbridge is a colourful, lively town with an abundance of fabulous independent boutiques, pubs, restaurants and food shops, making it a special place for a day's shopping. There are regular craft, food and vintage markets on Market Hill and a visit to the Woodbridge Shuck, a superb annual seafood festival, is a must.

The Newmarket Stallion by Marcia Astor and Allan Sly was erected in 2000 in recognition of the part Newmarket has played in racing history. It is fittingly located on the roundabout leading to the town's two flat racecourses, the July Course and the Rowley Mile. The former schedules the summer racing, whereas the latter prides itself on its 'world-class facilities' and is the venue for the spring and autumn race meetings.

Suffolk is blessed with many nature reserves, all providing vital habitat for our wildlife and protected species. The stunning wetland of RSPB Lakenheath Fen in the northwest of the county does just this. Bearded tits, bitterns, sedge warblers and cranes are just some of the birds to be spotted. In spring and summer, there is a healthy population of these small tortoiseshell butterflies, for whom the yellow flowers of ragwort are an important source of nectar.

June sees Sudbury Freemen's Common burst into colour with the vibrant yellow of buttercups. These ancient water meadows are carefully managed by the Sudbury Common Lands Charity, whose trustees play a crucial role in maintaining the habitat of an array of flora and fauna now otherwise rare in Suffolk. In keeping with ancient traditions, chemicals are never used here and the land has never been ploughed. Summer grazing cattle are essential in maintaining the composition and structure of the land.

There was a crooked man,
and he walked a crooked mile.
He found a crooked sixpence
upon a crooked stile.
He bought a crooked cat,
which caught a crooked mouse,
And they all lived together
in a little crooked house.

The town of Lavenham allegedly inspired the above nursery rhyme. This is a reasonable assumption to make given the remarkable Crooked House on the High Street.

Not to be outdone by Captain's Wood, Arger Fen and Spouse's Vale Nature Reserve has an equally striking display of bluebells in spring. Its ancient woodland and fen meadow provide an important sanctuary for rare species, such as the barbastelle bat and the hazel dormouse. Managed by Suffolk Wildlife Trust, the reserve covers around 272 acres in the Sudbury area of the county.

In 1828, the Cock Inn on Polstead's village green was the scene of the inquest into the death of Maria Marten of the Red Barn Murder fame. Today, this seventeenth-century pub serves delicious, home-cooked food, afternoon and cream teas, as well as a large and varied selection of beverages. It is a popular stop for ramblers and cyclists and is well-frequented by villagers, given its location at the heart of the community.

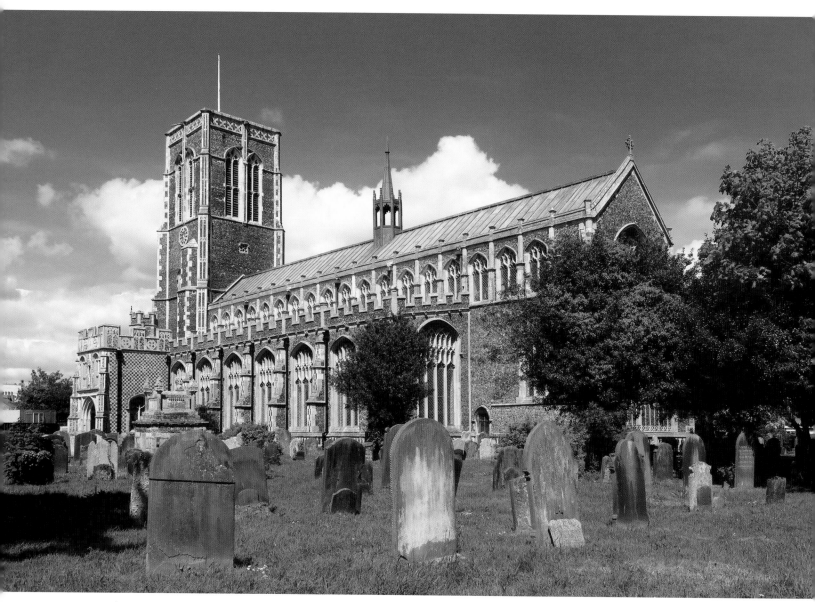

There is more to Southwold than sandy beaches and buckets and spades. The popular seaside resort has many historic buildings. The remarkable flint and stone church of St Edmund dates from the fifteenth century and replaces a thirteenth-century building destroyed by fire. The church is a typical Suffolk wool church and is just a stone's throw away from the lighthouse and brewery in the town centre.

Comprising river meadows, vast open stretches of heathland and enclosed clumps of woodland, Cavenham Heath National Nature Reserve in the Brecks is the epitome of tranquillity. Rare birds such as the nightjar and woodlark nest here and it is home to a population of adders. In summer, the Heath is alive with colour as the heather begins to bloom. There is arguably no better place to feel at one with nature.

It is impossible to overlook the Newmarket Clock Tower at the top end of the town's High Street. It was built by Richard Arber and funded by the inhabitants of the town to mark the Golden Jubilee of Queen Victoria; an opening ceremony was held in 1890. The clock inside was a donation from a local horse trainer and it requires 115 turns to wind it manually once a week.

The colourful Port of Felixstowe, viewed here across the water from Shotley Point, is the UK's largest container port. Around three thousand ships pass through the docks annually, confirming the key role it plays in facilitating the country's trade. As a leading port, it is capable of welcoming the world's largest container ships, like the OOCL Hong Kong that docked here for the first time in 2017. Pictured is a Maersk line ship.

46, Gainsborough Street, Sudbury, was once the childhood home of Thomas Gainsborough, who was born in the town in 1727. His parents purchased the house for £230 in 1722. Since the 1950s, it has belonged to the Gainsborough's House Society, who bought the house with the aim of turning it into a centre dedicated to the great artist. This excellent museum continues to evolve today.

These cute Greyface Dartmoor lambs are bred at Baylham House Rare Breeds Farm near Needham Market in Mid Suffolk. Baylham describes itself as 'a small livestock farm breeding farm animals that were once common, but are now very rare'. The rare breeds farm is very much a working farm, but with so many animals to discover and feed, it is a wonderful place for a family day out.

Bright yellow rapeseed fields are a common sight in May in the colourful patchwork of Suffolk countryside. Suffolk farmers often dedicate their fields to rapeseed due to the growth in popularity of its oil, viewed by many as a healthier, less expensive substitute for olive oil. This field was photographed on the outskirts of Bury St Edmunds.

Undoubtedly the most famous residents of Beyton, these white geese wander freely on the village green, occasionally bringing the traffic to a halt.

Wild poppies often add a touch of colour to Suffolk roadsides when they spring up at random in the early summer months. Occasionally, ramblers are lucky enough to stumble across a whole field of them, like this one on the banks of the River Orwell.

The atmospheric ruins of Leiston Abbey are tucked away in the tranquillity of the east Suffolk countryside. The original Abbey was founded in 1182 near Minsmere, but constant flooding led to its relocation to Leiston in the fourteenth century. Excavations at the Abbey in 2014 revealed the skeleton of an enormous dog. Were these the remains of the Black Shuck, who allegedly travelled across the East of England terrifying and in some cases killing the locals in the sixteenth century?

The River Orwell meets the River Stour at Shotley Gate, where the saltmarshes and mudflats are an important environment for waterfowl and wading birds. Once a rarity in Britain, little egrets are now more commonly seen in this area. Shotley was the first place in Suffolk to gain 'Walkers are Welcome' accreditation, thanks to Shotley Open Spaces, a volunteer group working tirelessly to 'preserve and protect communal outdoor spaces' in the community.